First Edition: 2018   **Second Edition:** 2022

Authored & Published by: Bellamkonda K. Kishore
nephron369@yahoo.com   www.bkkishore.online

© 2019 B.K. Kishore: All rights are reserved. Copyright Registration No. TXu 2-102-719

The text in this book is copyright protected. It is strictly prohibited to reproduce this book or in parts either in print or in digital form or by xerox or in any other means without the prior permission of the author. Translation of this book into any other language is also prohibited. However, genuine proposals to translate this book into other languages will be considered.

Reference to be used while citing from this book with copyright permission:
Kishore BK, *In*: Tamasoma Jyothirgamaya, Second Edition, 2022, page no. xx, Sandy, Utah, USA ISBN: xxxxxx

This book is dedicated to Sri Sathya Sai Baba, whose Divinity has influenced my life and guided me – Author

ISBN 979-8-98-636040-9

9 798986 360409

Price: US$12 Paperback & US$5 Kindle

Profits from sale of this book will go to SAI Kuteer, a 501 (C) 3 charity, Sandy, Utah, USA http://saikuteer.org

From the Pen of the Author

Thank you for reading my book. "Education should be man-making", so said Swami Vivekananda. But these days it is hard to find such education in any country. What we consider as education today is nothing but imparting knowledge, skills, and abilities to make a living. Degrees have lost their value as a sign of intellectual maturity and wisdom. Often, they serve as licenses to earn money. In this process students and young people are getting confused and lost. They are facing crossroads at every turn of their lives and find no clues or help with which way to turn. Added to this, right from the elementary school until they leave the universities, they are expected to just imbibe "information", with no coaching or help in navigating through the complexities of their lives. It is similar to sending a soldier with sophisticated firearms to fight with the enemy on the mountains, with no training in mountain combat. The result is that even the most highly educated youth often get lost in this world. Even if they succeed in their professions, they do not know how to derive happiness in their life.

This book results from my life-long efforts to learn about life, and pass on whatever I learned to others, especially the younger generations, so they can be benefitted. They are often under the impression that times have changed and so they must change the way they think and act. That is not always true. Certain things about life do not change with time. One of them is Sanathana Dharma or the eternal principles governing the humans and their destiny. The Sanathana Dharma is based on five pillars – Satya (Truth), Dharma (Right Conduct), Santhi (Peace), Prema (Love), and Ahimsa (Non-violence). The other thing that does not change with time is Swadharma or one's duty based on one's inherent nature and propensities. These two aspects that govern human life are presented in two chapters of this book. Believe me, whatever unrest, and chaos we are witnessing today in the world, be it at the individual or family or community or national or international level, it can be traced to the fall of humanity from these two great principles given to it a long time ago. Time may change, social fabric may change, culture may change, but humanity must cling on to these two principles to maintain harmony, peace, and prosperity. If we go back and search, most messiahs and prophets or avatars propagated these two principles. That shows the eternal nature and value of these two principles.

If the world has to change and humanity has to survive, there is no way other than individual transformation by moving from darkness to light (*Tamasoma Jyothirgamaya*). And darkness vanishes automatically when we light up a lamp in our hearts. Please send your feedback to the author at nephron369@yahoo.com.

Bellamkonda K. Kishore, M.D., Ph.D., MBA
Academician, Innovator & Entrepreneur
Sandy, Utah, United States

www.bkkishore.online

Dr. Vadrevu K. Raju, M.D., FARS, FACS

Founder and President, Eye Foundation of America, Morgantown, WV
Clinical Professor of Ophthalmology, West Virginia University, Morgantown, WV
Chairman, Gautami Eye Institute, Rajahmundry, AP, India
http://www.eyefoundationofamerica.org/

    I am honored to write foreword for Kishore's hard work "Tamasoma Jyothirgamaya" (from darkness lead me to light). He painstakingly compiled the book and brought to us knowledge, wisdom, and age-old philosophy of India.

    In his brief book, he brings to our conscious, the penetrating words like Faith, Truth, Fate, Destiny, and much more perplexing words like Swadharma and Paradharma. At the same time, he brings to us great quotes from Abraham Lincoln, Albert Einstein, Bill Gates, Warren Buffett, and many other luminaries.

    The reader shouldn't miss the starfish story and "Diamond and Graphite."

    After reading and rereading this magnificent little book, I am reminded of a quote by great Indian statesman and philosopher, Sir Sarvepalli Radhakrishnan. "Human nature is fundamentally good, and the spread of enlightenment will abolish the wrong."

    I congratulate Dr. Bellamkonda Kishore for bringing out such a valuable book.

Dr. Malireddy S. Reddy,
BVSc (DVM), M.S., Ph.D.
President & CEO
American Dairy and Food Consulting Laboratories, Inc. (ADFAC)
&
International Media and Cultures, Inc. (IMAC), Denver, CO
http://www.askimac.com/

This book entitled *Tamasoma Jyothirgamaya* by Dr. B.K. Kishore is outstanding and a great gift to the humans of all walks of life. I know Dr. Kishore well and I have always admired him for his worldly practical knowledge regarding the divine and the purpose of humans on this earth. Humans are the only ones with a developed central nervous system a brain with over 100 billion cells. Unfortunately, the full potential of the human brain is not tapped to come up with brilliant ideas which can solve the worldly problems, specifically to improve the peace. Dr. Kishore eloquently interpreted the meaning of Sanathana Dharma in simplified words. Unless we follow and practice these five elements of Sanathana Dharma i.e., Sathya, Dharma, Santhi, Prema and Ahimsa, our chances of having peace in our lives or in the world is next to impossible.

Another brilliant aspect of Dr. Kishore's book, which I like much, is the explanation he offered to distinguish Swadharma form Paradharma. He has interpreted the genesis of Swadharma in the form of a seed which has all the past knowledge from previous life, which can be further expanded in the present life. In essence, if someone fulfills his Swadharma in the current life, he/she can excel in life or profession with true happiness. If someone interfered or obstructed that person from practicing or implementing the inherent Swadharma and directed that person's path into Paradharma for the monetary or worldly benefits, then he/she will never become an outstanding individual and for sure will not be a happy soul. Dr. Kishore is not only an MD, Ph.D., and MBA by education, but also a humanitarian and a philosopher.

Dr. Kishore is very much concerned about the youth suicides in India, and he has apparently isolated the principal cause of these unpleasant suicides. According to him the core cause of these suicides may be because of pressure from parents and the society trying to push the youth to take up Paradharma rather than practicing Swadharma. In simple words, if a student has inherent seed of passion in biological sciences (due to Swadharma), rather than having him/her pursue the career in biological sciences, the parents and/or society may force him/her into other monetarily attractive professions (Paradharma). By following Paradharma just to fulfill his/her obligations to the parents or succumbing to societal pressures (e.g., marriage prospects), a student can never be exceptional in the Paradharma and will stay as a mediocre for the rest of his/her life. Ultimately, he/she gets depressed. In certain cases, this depression will lead to anxiety and fear, which ultimately result in dissolution of life. Although no studies are available, this could be the principal reason for the high suicide rate in young people in India. In my opinion, Dr. Kishore is the only scientist and philosopher who had come up with a potential cause of these youth suicides in India. According to him, although 5,000 years ago Lord Krishna had pointed out the importance of practicing Swadharma to depressed King Arjuna in the battleground (Kurukshethra), however, the significance of this message has not been communicated to the general public in India.

I strongly recommend to all the people, irrespective of their religion or belief, to read Dr. Kishore's book and practice the principles he has outlined to improve peace and harmony in the world with love and empathy. We can never be appreciated by God if we do not take care of the needs of the helpless people since all people are children of God.

Sri Mahadev Desai

Journalist and Prolific Writer, Atlanta, GA
http://www.atlantadunia.com/dunia/News09/mahadev_desai.htm

I consider myself blessed and honored to write these few lines of a Foreword to Dr. Bellamkonda Kishore's inspirational and motivational *'Tamasoma Jyothirgamaya'* (from darkness to light); a collection of well-researched, insightful, thought-provoking, and illuminating essays, in easy to read and lucid style. I have been fortunate to have known Dr. Kishore over the past several years as we share our writings and interest in spiritual matters. He is a medical scientist and lives in Sandy, a suburb of Salt Lake City, Utah, United States. He is an international speaker and an ardent follower of Sri Sathya Sai Baba.

In this book, he shares his insights and wisdom through his essays on various personal life values that can help one realize his/her full potential as an individual. The author has written on The Power of Faith; Fate and Destiny; Living with a Purpose; Value-added Life; Human Creative Power; Creating and Sustaining Balance—Integrating Professional, Family and Social Life; Love and Compassion; Sanathana Dharma; and Swadharma vs. Paradharma. In addition to these engaging and thoughtful essays, the book also has well-composed poems, 'The Crisis of Inner Faith' and 'Live Like the Lotus'. The essays and the poems have the added sparkle of captivating pictures and quotations by exemplary figures like Mother Teresa; Mahatma Gandhi; Buddha; Albert Einstein, Abraham Lincoln; Ralph Waldo Emerson; Nobel Peace Prize winner Prof. Muhammad Yunus, to name a few.

The author urges everyone to be loving, compassionate and empathetic and strive to make a difference, however small or insignificant it may appear to be. And in his last two essays, he stresses that even though times have changed, one must not abandon the principles of Sanathana Dharma and Swadharma to ensure harmony, peace, and prosperity. I heartily recommend this book of enriching life lessons to all.

The Power of Faith

Photo by Zac Durant on Unsplash

We have all heard the word faith. But what does it really mean? There are many versions of what faith means. Perhaps the best one I ever heard is "*faith is believing in what we do not see today; the reward of faith is one day we will see what we believe*". Believing in what we do not see today is really the toughest part for many of us.

It is because, most of us do not believe even in what we see right now. History of mankind has proven time and again that for a person of faith who nurtures it ardently, there is no defeat or failure on earth, although such a person may face innumerable difficulties and obstacles in nurturing his/her faith on a constant basis. For instance, Satya Harichandra had immense faith in Truth. Although he lost his kingdom and got separated from his family members, he ardently nurtured his faith without wavering even for a second. And he won at the end. That is why we call Satya Harichandra a benchmark for Truth even today, several thousands of years after he left this planet.

Similarly, the Pandava brothers, especially Arjuna, had immense faith in Lord Krishna. Arjuna had so much faith in Krishna, he was ready to do anything that Krishna asked him to do, even if that needed giving up his life. His immense faith in Lord Krishna was clearly evident when he went to Dwaraka seeking Krishna's help in the upcoming war at Kurukshetra. Krishna offered him a choice. The choice of himself alone never handling a weapon in the battlefield, or his entire army, cavalry, war elephants, and others. Arjuna had Krishna alone rejecting the entire army of Krishna, against which he and his brothers had to eventually fight by default. Any prudent and pragmatic person in the worldly sense would have chosen the army of Krishna, instead of choosing lone and non-fighting Krishna. But, the prudence or pragmatism did not dictate the choice made by Arjuna. It was his faith in Lord Krishna, whom he believed from the depth of his heart as the incarnation of Lord Vishnu. That made Arjuna to choose Krishna in preference to his entire army against which he eventually fought and won. **Thus, faith is far superior to prudence, or pragmatism.** Unlike prudence and pragmatism which are the products of a sharp, yet self-defeating, intellect, faith originates deep in the soul and is expressed through the heart in a Divine fashion. From the point of worldly sense, it may appear inferior to reasoning. But it defies and rises above reasoning. *It is because faith transcends intellectual debate and reasoning.*

This brings us to the point - intelligence versus faith. Does it mean intelligent people have less faith? Not necessarily. But intelligent people, who consider themselves very prudent and pragmatic, may often be led by the strategic or logistic aspects of an issue or choice. That makes them i g n o r e or not recognize the potential "power of faith". There are always exceptions, just like with Arjuna with a sharp intellect, and who was a strong warrior, but was led by his faith in Lord Krishna. *That surrendering one's intellect, power, might, valor and every virtue in the worldly sense, to faith in the Almighty. The outcome of such a phenomenon, which is well described in Bhagawad Gita as Jnana Karma Sanyasa Yoga, is the supreme way of living on this planet according to our scriptures.*

Our ancestors, who ardently practiced such type of Yoga of supreme faith and sacrifice, reaped the best in both worlds - the one on this planet and the other in the heaven. By doing so, they created and nurtured a very rich culture unparalleled in the annals of history of mankind. They passed on those jewels to us to preserve and take care. But we failed them by spilling the jewels on the floor and walking on them day and night. The result is, as a culture we, are not the best in this world anymore. We may try to defend our culture by talking about it all the time and feeling great about the great virtues of our ancestors or our past glory. That is comparable to picking up each pearl fallen on the floor and praising how great it was when it was in the necklace. But by doing so, we cannot restring the necklace. Because the thread that holds the precious pearls is missing. Unless we find that missing thread called Faith, we cannot restore our cultural glory.

We need faith by all means and at all levels. We need to rekindle faith first in ourselves, in the Almighty, in our family, in our kith and kin, in our neighbors, in our community and in the destiny of our lands, the motherland or the adopted land. Then only the future of our children, grandchildren and great grandchildren will be assured of peace, harmony, and happiness.

But by using our so-called prudence and pragmatism, we can take care of our needs on this earth, we can educate our children, take care of their financial needs and future and then retire. But will that assure a great future for our children? Those of us who have lived on this planet and watched at least three generations of people here will agree with me, if I say that with each generation we have moved away from the essentials of faith and become more materialistic and short-sighted in our lives. We have lost passion, patience, and the ability to lead more meaningful and purpose-driven lives. We have moved away from real happiness of associating with people and moved towards transient pleasures of material life. We h a v e lost our ability to deep-dive into Ananda or true happiness, and we are stuck with superficial surf called 'pleasures'. Unlike our forefathers, who used to possess things at their command, we are possessed by our own possessions. How can we derive true happiness even in the material sense, when we are possessed by things, with no control over them? This is all because of lack of faith in ourselves.

So, obviously the solution for all these anomalies lies in developing and nurturing faith in oneself. How? Faith is not something that one can find outside. It is there always within every one of us. Without faith life is impossible. It is a question of just manifesting it by constant attention and practice. It is similar to the skills we use and practice in our profession - be an engineer or surgeon or any profession. Without faith in what we do, what we think and what we say, we cannot even earn our bread and butter. So, we constantly nurture and improve our skills in work to move upwards. So, also, we need to nurture, manifest, and improve the faith in ourselves, in the people and community we live in. If we do that then developing faith in the Almighty is just a question of time.

But instead of doing that, those of us who recognize faith as a powerful thing in our lives, try to move the other way. They start with faith in the Almighty and ignore the community. They do not believe even their own kith and kin or family members. The result of this kind of faith is that it does not allow for manifestation of itself. It cannot be true faith. *It is because true faith does not create barriers. Faith is an absolute entity. Like truth, it has the power of breaking through all barriers.* Please recall, some of the greatest manifestations of faith from our scriptures, such as - Prahlada, who believed in the omnipresence of Vishnu in the pillar, and Meera, who drank poison sent by her husband with absolute faith in Lord Krishna. The greatest virtue of these people of faith is that they did not look at the Almighty with faith and ignored or disrespected the people adverse to them. The power of their faith was so vast, that it dwarfed any harm caused by their adversaries. This can happen only if one develops and nurtures the faith in its true form. This is the litmus test for us all to test our own faith in the Almighty. If we believe in the Almighty, then nothing in this world, however adverse it may be, should hurt us or even shake us. But if we are shaken by every adverse condition, then our faith is not matured, or solidified. It is superficial like the surf on the ocean.

One can raise a question here: What is the use of a strong faith in this world? May be it is useful for an Ascetic or Himalayan Yogi. But that solid faith is what is needed to achieve great things and attain great heights even in today's materialistic world. For instance, when Mother Theresa started her Sisters of Charity, she was alone without a central aid from the mission she was associated with. She did not have money or a place to work or people to help her. But she had one thing that can bring all these and much more - solid faith in the Almighty. She knew there is nothing in this material world not within the purview of God. If God wishes, He can bless us with every material thing in a no time. Lord Krishna did that for Kuchela, his poor childhood friend. *But all the riches in this world put together cannot buy even an inch of the Almighty. That is the greatest principle we all need to understand and respect.* Not understanding this great principle reflects a sign of one's own weakness and spiritual bankruptcy. What can such people do on this earth to make a difference? Perhaps only leading a life that does not affect the people, the community, or the society they live in. Do we want such life, however comfortable it may be?

Even the lives of very successful people, such as Nobel Laureates like Marie Curie, are full of faith. Marie Curie hailed from a poor family in Poland. Her father could not afford to send her to a college. But she believed in herself and determined to be a physicist. She worked hard, often without enough food to eat. But she earned a Ph.D. in Physics in France, the first ever awarded to a woman in France in those days. Eventually her faith and dedicated work led her to win, not one, but two Nobel Prizes. She was the first woman to win a Nobel, and the first person to receive two Nobel Prizes. Thus, even scientists have faith in their work and abilities, despite the innumerable difficulties or uncertainties or hardships they face. Without that staunch faith and highly disciplined life, they could not have achieved what they did. **So, the concept of faith is compatible with the modern life**.

But we often see people who are not serious about nurturing and developing faith in the Almighty and/or the people around them. Some complain "you know I had so much faith in the Almighty, but he never helped me". What do you mean by that? First, one must understand that faith is not something that we should cultivate in a conditional manner. **Faith should be followed unconditionally**. If we expect to be instantly rewarded with good fortune just by keeping faith for a certain period, then we are making a mockery of faith. Faith is not for trading with God in return for something beneficial in the material sense. It is not for bartering. **Faith is a Divine Principle**. It should not be degraded to mundane level to fit our needs. **Faith is a path to Divinity, Peace and Liberation**. But the byproducts of faith make our culture rich and noble. Not knowing these and expecting something miraculous to happen just because we have faith is only a sign of our ignorance at the best, or our foolishness at its worst.

Similarly, if we have faith in a person, then also it should be unconditional. You may wonder why? **Because, faith is a Divine Principle, and wherever we apply it, we need to respect the Divinity of it**. If we have that Divine faith in the people, it can change them for good even if they deviate from their path. Swami Vivekananda once said, "If I have a companion who believes me and loves me even if I turn to a devil tomorrow, then the power of such a faith will transform even the devil in me into an angel". Out of such faithful companionship a man may find liberation. The most important thing here is to understand that when a Divine Principle, such as the faith is sincerely and ardently applied, it has the power of transforming even the devil into an angel. **The power manifests out of our respect for that Divine Principle**. There is a nice parable for this from our scriptures. There was a guru with a few disciples. The guru was good, but he was not a highly evolved soul. But one of his disciples, an ardent student, had a higher level of Divine faith in his guru. One day, as the disciple was coming home from the woods, the water level in the canal which used to be knee-deep rose considerably to cross by walking through it. And there was no other mode of transportation to cross the culvert. So, the disciple invoked his Divine faith in his guru, and by constantly reciting his guru's name, he walked on the water without being drowned. While he was crossing the culvert by just walking on the surface of it, his guru saw that. When the disciple reached the shore, he bowed and touched the feet of his guru as a sign of gratitude. The surprised guru asked his disciple how he could do that. The disciple told him that by invoking the faith in his guru and He tried to test it by attempting to walk on the surface of the water by reciting his own name. Immediately he was drowned in the water. So, what made the disciple to do something great, which his guru could not do? Definitely it was not the power of the guru. Nor was it the power of his name. But it was the Divine faith that the disciple ardently nurtured and developed that gave him the power to walk on the water. Such is the power of faith, which unfortunately we have forgotten and so we cannot cultivate or nurture it and thus derive the immense benefits of it.

The above parable brings us to another point. It is not really whom we worship or follow, but the depth of our Divine faith ultimately helps us and guides us. So, let us all cultivate, nurture, and develop such Divine faith and make our lives noble, and thus help to restore past glory of our rich culture.

Where there is FAITH, there is LOVE.
Where there is LOVE, there is PEACE.
Where there is PEACE, there is GOD.
Where there is GOD, there is BLISS.

- Sri Sathya Sai Baba

The Crisis of Inner Faith

Photo by JJ Thompson on Unsplash

In a world that is full of flux
Where change is the only thing constant
Man must find his destiny
Despite the high odds of missing, it often…
Whether he likes it or not
One day or other he must resign
To accept the reality of the changing world
And look for peace and happiness inside…

However long it may take
For him to acknowledge the truth
That the only thing he can change
To stop the flux in his mind
Is nothing but his own attitude
And his own outlook to the changing world

From the dawn of the civilization
Great men and women consistently
Found and vouchsafed the truth
That the only thing to be conquered
To attain eternal peace and happiness
Is just within us and nowhere else…

When you stop trying to change others, and work on yourself,
your world changes for the better.
- Buddha

Fate and Destiny

What is Fate? Fate and destiny, the most powerful things in our lives, are two entities. But they are often confused with each other. Fate falls upon us, often without our invitation or thought of it. It can be good or bad from our perspective of view. According to the Karma theory fate is always related to our past actions, either in this or previous lives. We often fall prey to the fate in our lives – good or bad. If it is good, we enjoy it to the extent we often forget our responsibilities and obligations. If it is bad, we feel sad and expressed and often curse the whole world.

Destiny and Free Will: While fate mercilessly pushes us and appears to be beyond our control, however, the destiny is different. Destiny is something we can use to shape our lives, despite the fate that has fallen on us. While fate is what we get in our lives, destiny represents the "free will" that God blessed with every one of us to overcome the effect of fate. It may sound absurd. But it is true. God does not wish we should fall prey to our fateand hole up in dark corners of our lives until we die. Among all living creatures, only the humans are blessed with a "free will" to change their destiny.By exercising his/her free will a person can become an angel or a demon in this very life. What is this "free will" and how it equips us with the power to alter our destiny? Imagine you have been thrown by "fate" into a closed ring where there is a bull ready to attack you and gore you into pieces with its horns. Under such circumstances, you have two choices – either panic and run like a mad person in the ring and eventually get gored into pieces by the bull or stay calm and try to distract the bull from attacking you with some object and meanwhile find an opportunity to exit the ring quietly. Similarly, God has blessed man with all the will and skills necessary to overcome the fate. Most of us do not realize this, and often lament about the fate and curse the world. We feel we are inherently and permanently trapped in a hole from where we can never escape, and so we dig more. *But the wisdom teaches us that when we find ourselves trapped in a hole, the first thing we have do is stop digging more*.

How to Conquer the Fate? Fate cannot be conquered by lamenting about it, just like one cannot escape from a hole by digging more. Fate is conquered by deliberate attempts to exercise our will and to use our skills, just like the one trapped in a hole tries to climb the muddy walls, however slippery they may be. To understand this, one needs deep contemplation and the ability to delve into one's own mind. There comes the importance of cultivating the knowledge about one's own self, the so-called self-knowledge, which our scriptures have been advocating since time immemorial. But we spend little or no serious time to understand our own inner self. We explore the whole town or city we live to find more places of fun or entertainment. But we do not make serious attempts to explore our own inner selves. But the irony is we live – day and night – in our inner selves, not outside. We live in our minds round the clock. Even when walking around the town or a mall, we live in our minds. There is no fun in the town or the mall unless our minds are inclined to have fun. Then why should we waste our precious God-given lives, minds and time on things that do not belong to us in any way? *It is because we lost ourselves. We are constantly searching for ourselves outside, which we will never find*. There is a nice and well-known parable. The king of a country lost his mind and went on searching his whole kingdom to find out who was ruling his kingdom. The result, he never found the king. Similarly, we should not lose our inner kingdom and look for happiness, peace, and purpose in the external world.

Summoning the Hidden Powers within Us: Swami Vivekananda said: "All the strength and succor you need to be successful in this world are within you only." Every human, however small and weak he/she may appear or feel, is endowed with an infinite amount of hidden power. How can we summon the hidden power within us? *It is just being aware of the hidden power within oneself*. The more we are conscious of the hidden power within us, the more of it manifests itself to the physical level. It is like the sweet water in a deep well in our backyard. If we ignore the sweet water in our own deep well and go after the attractive mirages everywhere else on the surface of earth because they are more accessible, then we can never quench our thirst. We only face disappointment and despair in life.

How to Shape our Destiny? Now, coming back to the destiny, what it means to us? How to focus and shape our own destiny? Well, first we need to understand that every one of us comes into this world with a clear God-given blueprint in life. Whether we are born low or high in terms of economic or social standards of this physical or rather mundane world, God has a definite blueprint for all of us, which is custom-made to suit each one of us. However, instead of giving the blueprints directly to us, God hides them on the path of our life's journey, and watches how we discover them, read them and interpret them. If we have that faith in God, then we will find our custom-made blueprints in our lives. Most miseries and misfortunes we face in our lives are due to not finding or do not trying to find out the God-given and custom-made blueprints in our lives. Some of us, after an initial finding of the blueprints, deliberately destroy them just because they could not understand them properly or they just do not like the way the blueprints are leading them in their lives. And then they try to prepare their own blueprints with their limited mind, limited wisdom, limited knowledge, and short-sightedness. *The hard reality is however perfect the blueprints in life we make may appear to us, they are no match for the ones that God has made for us at the time of our birth.*

God not only made a blueprint for every one of us, but he also blessed with the same time scale for all of us to work on those blueprints in our lives.

We may have been born rich or poor or very healthy or less healthy or physically strong or not. But we all have the same scale of time. The clock ticked the moment we were born, and our lives keep on moving in one direction only - forward. **Time is the only thing in this world, which when lost, cannot be recovered**. We can lose wealth or health and recover them either partially or fully. But when a minute of our lives is gone, it is gone forever.

All these illustrate one thing. ***Our lives are as rich and meaningful as we want them to be.*** It is that simple. No one is putting a barricade or barrier to find the God-given blueprints and thus make "real progress" in our lives, except our mind, and our small thinking and our inability to see things in their true perspective. Swami Vivekananda declared: "Man is not bound by anything in this world, except the ones which he imposes on himself." That is true. For instance, while persuading the masses to burn the Manchester-made garments and wear home-spun Khadi during the Swadesi movement, Mahatma Gandhi said: Spin the cloth with home-grown cotton and wear it with dignity, however small it may be, just like I do. Looking at the scantily clad Mahatma Gandhi, Winston Churchill called him "Naked Fakir of India". But that did not deter Gandhi. Mohandas Karamchand Gandhi was born rich, educated in England and became an attorney. He went to South Africa to become a successful lawyer and earn riches. But he did not pursue that path for long. Instead, fighting for the rights and freedom of the oppressed masses, he transformed himself into Mahatma (Great Soul), who gave up all his riches and wore a small cloth of Khadi that barely covered his body. Yet he proudly wore that piece of cloth as a symbol of poverty among the masses of India, who live in 700,000 villages and hardly could eat a meal a day. There are other such great people, like Mother Theresa, Abraham Lincoln, Martin Luther King, Jr., and Nelson Mandel, who found their God-given blueprints in their lives. Such were the noble souls that walked in flesh and blood on this earth.

The difference between these great souls and us is only one thing. Although they were born ordinary, had no gifted skills, they genuinely struggled to discover the blueprints that God has custom-prepared for them. And once they found their God-given blueprints, they stuck to those plans, leaving aside all their whims and fancies in life. During that process they transformed and conquered their own minds and realized the greatness in following the God-given blueprints in life. They understood the ultimate value of following the God-given blueprints leaving their personal feelings about them. They understood the sublime God-given path to follow and gave up their own little paths in life. We need to understand the lives of such great persons like Abraham Lincoln, Mahatma Gandhi, and Mother Theresa. Then only we can find deeper meaning and purpose in our lives. Then only we can become scuba divers in our lives, diving deep into the ocean and finding the real wealth and riches. Otherwise, we will remain as surfers in our lives. Surfers depend always on the waves powered by the winds to rise and fall for their sport. Unlike a scuba diver who deliberately chooses his/her path under the water, a surfer never finds the real path, except floating on the waves on the surface of the ocean. A scuba diver finds the real wealth on the seabed, and a surfer gets only the froth.

Attitude is the Key for Everything in Life: Finally, the above narration brings us to the most important aspect of human life: **The Attitude**. *Attitude is the key for everything in life.* We may or may not be born fortunate enough. But that is only a part of our lives. If our birth represents the fate with which we are born, then our attitude shapes our destiny in this world. Fate and destiny are two entities. Fate is not in our hands, but attitude which can shape our destiny is in our hands. Smart people know how to tread their lives in this world without being affected by their fate at birth or the fate they have to encounter in their lives. We all have our free will to exercise, and some of us do it wisely and some do not. And fate or fortune or intelligence have nothing to do with that. *It is simply an attitude problem.* Those who are fortunate enough to have a better start should realize how fortunate they are and thus thank God. Those who are less fortunate, should thank God for the hardship which inculcates discipline and thus makes them realize the value of human life and relationships. The less fortunate need not worry about their fate at birth. Instead, they should emulate the life of a lotus flower. It is born in mud and slime at the bottom of the pond infested with frogs, fishes, snails, and leeches. But it grows straight up and holds its head high above water, looking towards the Sun (read Almighty). It refuses to get wet although the muddy water is the basis for its life. Although the frogs, fishes, snails, and leeches have been co-habiting the pond with the lotus flower, they may never realize the beauty of a lotus flower. It is the hard-working bees and beautiful butterflies from far off regions that flock to a blossoming lotus flower and enjoy its beauty and sweetness of its nectar. We can all emulate the life of a lotus flower and become great. *There is nothing in this world to stop us from doing so. Except our attitude!*

You have it in your power to make your days on Earth a path of flowers, instead of a path of thorns. – Sri Sathya Sai Baba

Men are not prisoners of fate, but only prisoners of their own minds.
- *Franklin D. Roosevelt*

You either get bitter or you get better. It is that simple. You either take what has been dealt to you, and allow it to make you a better person, or you allow it to tear you down. That choice does not belong to fate, it belongs to you. – Josh Shipp

The only person you are destined to become is the person you decide to be.
- Ralph Waldo Emerson

Live Like the Lotus

Lotus, the beautiful flower
Is born in mud and slime
At the bottom of the pond
But it grows straight up
Holding its head high above water
Looking at the bright Sun
It refuses to get wet
Although it sustains on water

The frogs and fishes in the water
The snails and leeches in the slime
Which spend all their time in gobbling
With no other purpose in their lives
Never understand the beauty of the Lotus
But the Lotus is not concerned
Because it knows well
That the moment it blossoms
It can attract far better beings
Which flock to it from far of regions
The hardworking bees
Collecting nectar to make honey
That keeps humans healthy
And the colorful butterflies
Which pollinate the flowering plants
While they sip tiny droplets of nectar
And thus help the nature to nurture
Bees and butterflies both show
Higher purpose in their lives
They know the beauty of the Lotus
And enjoy its sweet nectar
While serving the nature and humanity

We have to live like the Lotus
In this world, during our lives
Without getting entangled
But rising above the mundane
And paying no attention
To those mundane people
Who can never understand our values
But longing for those noble ones
That can appreciate our ideals and values

Nothing can stop us emulating the Lotus
And living high above the mundane world
It is our will that can make us a Lotus

Living with a Purpose

Photo by Aaron Burden on Unsplash

What is life? The answer depends on to whom we pose the question. If I ask you all to write down in one sentence what is life, perhaps there will be as many types of answers as the number of readers of this article. All those answers are the products of subjective assessment of each one of us. Obviously, they may or may not be the true representation of the life in a universally acceptable manner. So let us examine life from an objective angle that can be universal and verifiable.

If we apply objective assessment, we can come up with a definition of life that every one of us will agree. What if I say that *life is a one-way bridge which links birth and death?* One way in the sense, our lives at the physical plane move in one direction only - forward - although our minds can move back into the past and project into the future. I am sure this definition of life is acceptable to all. Having defined the life in a universally acceptable and objective fashion, now let us examine the purpose of life and then every component of this bridge, called life. A bridge has only one purpose - that is to help us cross something - a river or stream of water. Unlike an ordinary countryside road, no one wants to park his/her car for a while on the bridge. While crossing the bridge everyone seems eager to get to the other end of the bridge. Similarly, it is no one is foolish to camp on a bridge. We all know and agree that fact regarding a physical bridge. But with life, which is also a form of bridge we seem to forget the rules of the game and would like to stay on the bridge forever. It is true with every one of us.

Crossing the Bridge Smoothly: The next question is how to cross the bridge smoothly during our lifetime? Two things come to our aid - *direction and momentum*. Both are equally important. Momentum without proper direction may not lead us to our destiny. It is like sitting at the steering wheel of a 600 HP, 8.4 L and 10-cylinder Dodge Viper and hitting the highway with full throttle with no road map or GPS navigation system. The only thing one can derive from it is the nice handling of a car that can hit 60 mph under 3 seconds. But direction without momentum is useless. For instance, we can have a clear map of where we want to go, but we are stuck with a golf cart, not a car, then it will be frustrating. Both these scenarios are not ideal for smooth crossing of the bridge of life. So, to cross the bridge of life smoothly, we need both proper direction and reasonable momentum. Then we can relax as the rest is assured.

But unfortunately, most of us do not understand the logic of life and follow it. Why? The reasons for our failure to understand the logic of life may be many. But there are two that make us get stuck on the bridge for a long time. First, most of us do not realize that life is like a marathon, but not a 100 meters sprint that needs to be finished in a few seconds to win the race. In a 100 meters sprint we need speed more than anything else to win the race. But in a marathon, we need not rush or dash. Instead, we need to focus on the route and the pace, and adjust our performance in accordance with our capacity and endurance to run for a longer time. Our goal in a marathon is to finish the race successfully without collapsing on the way due to fatigue and exhaustion. Furthermore, in a marathon we need not bother about the pace of our fellow runners. *Most problems we face in our lives are due to our behaving as though we are on a series of 100 meters sprints in life, while we are on a marathon.* It is humanly impossible to run a series of 100 meters sprints covering the distance of a marathon of 10 to 20 miles. *The moment we realize this, then life opens to us in a very different dimension - much more vast, pleasant, and joyful.* In the marathon of life, we need to set our goals and pace depending on our inherent capacity, ability and perseverance. These goals should be realistic – neither too ambitious to attain nor too small to transform us into lazy people. Then we should cross the bridge of life without sacrificing our values in life, taking our own time, but moving steadily. Then crossing the bridge becomes a pleasant experience.

Sharing the Bridge with Others: Second, we need to cultivate the habit of giving back to this world and community constantly right from the very young age. We all come into this world with empty hands, and we are bound to leave this world with empty hands. So, the beginning balance is zero, and ending balance is zero. However, between the beginning and the ending balances, we have tremendous capacity to handle our accounts in three ways: (i) in a way that helps the community; (ii) in a way that deprives the community; or (iii) in a way there is no impact on the community. While depriving the community by messing up our accounts can be considered a vice, not having any impact on the community during our lives is not a virtue either. Sometimes I hear people boasting they are perfect because they do not expect a penny from others, and they do not give a penny to others. While not expecting a penny from others is a virtue, not giving a penny to others is not a virtue to boast of. *Not giving a penny to others is only a static form of life, which is born out of ignorance of the fluid dynamics of life. Life is a form of free-flowing energy.* The tendency of life is to flow always like a river. The flow gives beauty to the river, sustenance to its aquatic life, nourishment to the vegetation along its banks, and the majesty to the moving boats. By constructing a dam on a free-flowing river one can hold water in a large tank and elevate the level of river upstream of the dam. But the river becomes stagnant and loses all its beauty. A dam is an artificial structure built with a limited purpose. Construction of a dam may not always consider the collateral damage it may cause to ecosystem, flora and fauna along the river, and the lives of people who live along the river and depend on it for their livelihood. A dam has a real value only when the accumulated water is diverted into irrigation canals and over the turbines that produce electricity. Without these, the dam is only an ecologically damaging structure. *Similarly, accumulating wealth and prosperity during our lives even by good and* *fair means and not having a positive impact on the community is like a dam that holds water with no benefit to the people.*

But one can accumulate wealth and become prosperous, yet one can become a multipurpose dam – with an array of irrigation canals distributing water, generating electricity, taking care of the ecosystem around the dam in a sustainable fashion and protecting the flora and fauna that depend on the river, and finally relocating and rehabilitating the poor people who live along the river and depend on it for their sustenance. That is the way one must aspire to become prosperous in this world. It is because, during our struggles to become prosperous and wealthy, we invariably consume resources and manpower from this world. We rarely appreciate this. **Since we use resources and manpower from this world for our personal progress and prosperity, it is imperative on our part to pay back at least a part of those assets to this world.**

Crossing the Bridge with a Purpose: *Material wealth may not give real happiness in life unless it is matched with purity of purpose and values.* Another thing we rarely understand is that material advancement, however honestly it is pursued without sacrificing our values, does not bring true satisfaction in life unless we cultivate compassion and a tendency to give or share our wealth with the less fortunate children of the God. **We cannot expect God to be kind and compassionate to us as a father or mother unless we share our riches or our wealth with the less fortunate children of our Eternal Father or Mother.** In God's vision His less fortunate children are our own siblings or brothers and sisters. No parent will be happy to see only one or two of their children are wealthy and prosperous in life, while the rest are suffering from poverty and squalor. More than that, it will be very painful to the parents when they see that their rich and prosperous children turn their faces away from their less fortunate siblings. **So, God readily blesses those of His children who work for the welfare of the community, not just their own selves or their families.**

Winston Churchill said "You make a living with what you get. But you make a life with what you give". It is easier to make a living. These days anyone with a few skills, not as high as that of a surgeon or physician or lawyer or engineer, can have a decent living. But there are very few people in this world, who know how to make or build a life – the art of living. Without this art of living whatever wealth, we accumulate is like a warehouse or dumping ground for worthless goods – goods which cannot be displayed in show rooms. Only the art of living can equip us with a capacity to reduce the inventory in our warehouse and increase the assets that decorate our show rooms. The art of living can also convert our warehouse inventory into valuable intangible assets. **Finally, the brilliance of a diamond comes from the light it scatters, not the light it absorbs. So also, the value we generate in our lives comes from what we give to this world, but not what we take from it. So, let us shine like the diamonds.**

We can decorate the front yards of our houses with expensive, beautiful, and rare plants. That is fine. But it does not help beyond that. But if we can plant a tree on the roadside in a small village, under the shadow of which an exhausted farmer can rest for a while thrice blessed we are. *The yardstick that God uses to measure the purpose and values in our lives differs greatly from the one we use to measure our own lives.* I do not mean we should leave our lifestyles and give up all our wealth and become saintly people like Mother Theresa or Mahatma Gandhi. What I mean by the above is that while pursuing our earthly goals, we should simultaneously cultivate the habit of giving back to the community to whatever extent it is possible with a real feeling, compassion, and empathy in our hearts. The latter are very important, perhaps more than the amount we contribute. The earlier we start this in our lives, the better, even though the amount we invest is not high. It is like a long-term investment in a high-yielding guaranteed fund. *God responds to such selfless investments in His fund.* By investing in God's fund, I do not mean we should contribute to the Temples or Churches. What I mean is we should help the needy to whatever capacity we can. That is the real investment in God's fund. If we can invest one penny in His Eternal Fund, He will pay us back several folds higher than our investment. *There is no investment portfolio on earth that can match the God's Eternal Portfolio that never crashes and always yields high return.* He is very compassionate to His children who work for their siblings on the earth. So, we need not give up our lives or earthly goals. *We need to live with a purpose - much higher than our earthly goals and desires.* We need to cultivate a heart that is sensitive and responsive to the needs of our siblings on this earth. We should not turn our faces away from the needy and suffering, especially if we can help them, and thus seek the Blessings of the God. If we do not help, we are not only disappointing the needy person, but the very God we worship and seek compassion and love from.

Charity or material help should be complemented by true compassion, love, and humility. These are the qualities that God measures with His yardstick while approving the charitable acts of us. These are also the qualities that bring happiness and joy to the needy. The material help we may offer them only alleviates their suffering or satisfies their hunger. But it is the genuine heart-to-heart communication between us and the needy that transforms both parties and elevates them into higher realms of existence. That is the beauty of charity the world witnessed in Mother Theresa during her earthly sojourn. That is also the message of Bhagawad Gita, when Lord Krishna expounds the true meaning of Yajna to Arjuna. The day when we can perform such Yajna, the whole world turns into a joyful playground for us. We attain happiness and peace of mind while we are still on earth. Then we need not think of a heaven after death. Because, then we create a heaven of our own on this earth, which we readily share with others.

Thus, if happiness is the end point of life, we all desire, then there is no reason we should not appreciate that we can derive that happiness while crossing the bridge of life itself by cultivating a sublime purpose in our lives right from the beginning.

Hard work is painful when life is devoid of purpose. But when you live for
Something greater than yourself and the gratification of your own ego, then hard work becomes a labor of love.
- Steve Pavlina

Life is never made unbearable by circumstances, but only lack of meaning and purpose. - Victor Frankl

It is not enough to have lived. We should be determined to live for something. - Winston S. Churchill

Having a purpose is the difference between making a living and making a life. - Tom Thiss

Value-added Life

Photo by SHTTEFAN on Unsplash

What is Value-added Life? Whenever we invest our hard-earned money to buy a car, home, or property, we look at the value. We would like to see the initial quality, the long-term utility and re-sale or disposal value of it. We do look for "value" in everything we buy or acquire in our lives even though we know some of them may appreciate or depreciate over the time.

But we often forget that our lives also have value at birth, and the value of our lives may also appreciate or depreciate over time depending on how we lead our lives. *If there is anything in this world with a real value, it is only our lives*. Every other thing we acquire in life has only a "relative value" as compared to the value of our lives. The value of many material objects we acquire, such as a luxury car, may depreciate. But we can constantly increase the values of our lives. That is feasible and is in our own hands. While valuable goods and property we acquire can provide us comfortable life, they can never substitute the immense happiness and peace of mind that one can derive from a value-added life. Our scriptures emphasize the importance of value-added life or VAL. Our ancestors built the foundation of our culture on VAL. However, recently the cultural edifice of India is showing deep cracks due to lack of interest in the people to pursue a VAL. Here are some thoughts on how to develop and nurture a VAL and regain our lost glory, happiness, and peace in our lives.

How to Develop a Value-added Life (VAL)? First, we must assign certain core values to our lives based on our inherent or inner nature, not on the external world or its demands or expectations or temptations. To do this, we need to understand what our inherent nature, potentials, aptitude, and qualities are. Once we understand those, we need to relentlessly pursue them and build them inch by inch by dedication, constant practice, and application. If we keep on doing this, soon we will realize that the VAL will grow like a big tree within ourselves, bringing light and joy into our lives. Once these values are created and nurtured, then they will become the driving force within us to conquer aberrations that may cause frustration, depression, anxiety etc. Then we will become masters of our lives. We shape and lead our lives as we desire. Our lives will not be shaped or led by this world anymore. This de-links our minds from the aberrations generated by our worldly sojourn. The aberrations in our lives cannot be defeated by improving our external conditions alone, as they originate within us. Only a VAL can conquer and de-link them from our minds and thus keep us happy all the time. That is the meaning of life, even as per our Sanathana Dharma – *Dharma, Artha, Kama and Moksha*. All our sufferings are due to our failing to follow the Sanathana Dharma and thus break this order of life given to us by our great ancestors, and we expect to have a happy life. That is the paradoxical situation we are facing. The real solutions for the problems of our life are not as easy. They need deep thinking and contemplation and inner search. Whether we like it or not, that is the best way we can find the long-lasting answers to the problems of our lives.

The values we need to create and nurture in our lives are comparable to the value of a car we want to have. When we shop around for a great car, we look for a powerful turbo-charged engine with a high horsepower that can hit 0-60 mph in less than 6 seconds, traction control (TC), electronic stabilization system (EST), and anti-lock braking system (ABS), collision prevention system, and perhaps ten airbags supplemental restraining system (SRS). That is the minimum value we want to have for a vehicle we simply use to commute around the town, and we will keep for just for a few years only before trading it for a new car. There is nothing wrong in that. But we should translate such vision and values to our own lives. Unless we have turbo-charged high values, a good horsepower to propel us in the proper direction in life, a traction control to keep our intellectual grip a stabilization system that takes care of our mental balance through the adverse situations in our lives, an anti-locking system that prevents our mind being locked on unwanted issues, and virtues that can deploy like airbags in a crisis and protect us, and prevent collision our lives do not have more value than the car we drive around.

Be Focused and Clean in the Thought Process: Mind is like a computer. It functions efficiently when its memory is clean, and its hard drive is not cluttered with loose files in a disorganized fashion. Internally well-structured computers, protected by good anti-virus software and other programs, rarely crash. So also, the situation with the mind, which needs well-organized gray matter, anti-temptation software, pop-up blocker and a firewall to keep us protected and function efficiently. If one has all these, then there is no reason why one cannot be happy in his/her life.

Happiness is a State of Mind: Every religion, faith and scripture known to the mankind said this. But we still must realize it on our own. We cannot search for happiness outside like a commodity because it is already within us. We need to uncover it only. Take for instance when we were small children, we were happy all the time even though we possessed nothing. But as we grow older and older, as our possessions and attributes increase in number, we lose the happiness. Where did it go? Nowhere. We just covered it with our thought process, which goes outward looking for happiness in the external world. Our thoughts can be like the ashes that cover the burning cinders and thus make them look like extinguished. When we blow out the ashes, the burning cinders will be once again revealed. We should cultivate the habit of uncovering the happiness within and we should pursue our worldly goals. Then only the worldly goals will have great meaning for us. The external happiness we derive from our worldly goals or objectives is only a reflection of the happiness within us. Without that inner happiness, the external world has no meaning. So, the more we uncover the inner happiness, the more we can enjoy our lives – both personal and professional. Then the whole world looks like a playground for us to play happily.

We Should be Prepared to Sacrifice Smaller Things in Life to Achieve Greater Objectives: This is very important, especially if we want to achieve great objectives in life. We may set higher goals, have the potential to attain them, but if we are not willing or reluctant to sacrifice small or even petty things and cannot overcome over temptations, then we cannot achieve our goals. *Frustration is often the "difference" between what we want to achieve, and what we will sacrifice to achieve that.* We need to remember that nothing is easy or free in this world. We must earn everything we want to have in this life. Life will not be a bed of roses, or a cake walk. But that does not mean we do not have happiness in this life. We do have. But we need a balanced approach toward the dualities – gain and loss, pleasure and pain, joy and sorrow, riches, and rags. We need to develop equanimity of mind in life to face them. Then the mind is less fluctuating and more peaceful and powerful.

It is Never too Late to Change for the Better in our Life: It is never too late in our life to change for good. History of mankind is a proof for this statement. Emperor Ashoka who ruled India during the 1st century AD, started his life with a great ambition to conquer all the kings and acquire their kingdoms and thus become a Great Emperor. He fiercely fought many battles and won them. Finally in the battle of Kalinga, the toughest one he ever fought and won, he literally saw human massacre with blood flowing in streams. That changed his life forever. He became compassionate and embraced Buddhism and spread its gospel throughout the South Asia and the Far East, which changed the lives of hundreds of millions of people for good. He became a great ruler who worked for the welfare and happiness of his people. He erected great monuments and constructed shelters, hospitals, schools and other public facilities. Today, the pillar he erected in Saranath about two thousand years ago, the lion heads of which adore the official seal of the Republic of India, the largest democracy in the world, stands as an eternal proof that when one soul truly changes, it can do tremendous things in life, and can influence the lives of generations of people to come. Such is the power of the true change even it occurs late in the life. Similarly, Valmiki was born in a hunting tribe, but the sight of a bird lamenting for its fallen mate hit by a hunter's arrow changed him and made him a great sage, who composed Ramayana, one of the greatest epics of India. We may not be so great as Emperor Ahsoka or Sage Valmiki to do such great things by changing ourselves. But by changing for the better we can make a big difference in our small lives and in the lives of people around us. What else we want in our lives? **Every one of us must strive and do at least one good and great thing in our lives which will immensely benefit the people around us.** Then our lives have a lot of meaning and value to make us happy, especially when become older.

Each Person has Three Different Entities: Each one of us has three entities. The one we think about ourselves, the one that others think about us, and the third one – what we really are. The closer these three are the better will be our lives. But it is not an easy task and needs years of practice and contemplation. The easier one to achieve, with similar outcome is to keep the two – what we think of ourselves and what we really are as close as possible. This will allow us to be very realistic in our lives and thus make us happy and enjoy our lives. This only needs self-discipline and contemplation. This is my philosophy in life which I pursued for decades, and I found it works. Eventually I gained much from this perspective in life.

The value of life is not based on how long we live, but how much we contribute to others in our society.
- *Buddha*

Strive not to be a success, but rather to be of value.
- *Albert Einstein*

And, in the end, it's not the years in your life that count. It's the life in your years. - Abraham Lincoln

If your presence does not add value, your absence won't make a difference. - Zero Dean

The more we put helping others first…..and focus on adding value to other people's lives, the more abundance flows our way. It's a win-win all the way around.
- *Social Strategizer*

People who add value to others do so intentionally. I say that because to add value, leaders must give of themselves, and that rarely occurs by accident.
- *John C. Maxwell*

Love and Compassion

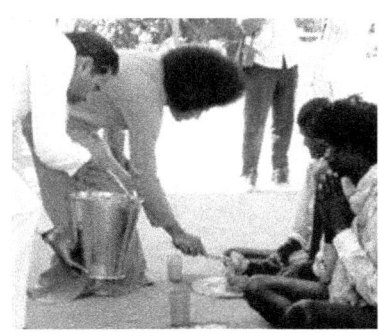

If in the future the world attains geopolitical stability, social justice, and economic equilibrium, with peace and happiness to all mankind, then the key driving force to reach that state will be **Love and Compassion**. But one may argue that the driving force(s) will be: Science and Technology; Globalization of the Economy; Spread of Democracy; Liberation from Social Injustice; and Universal Acceptance of Human Rights or a combination of the above. All these may be essential ingredients that set up the congenial atmosphere or platform needed to attain the stability, equilibrium, peace, and happiness in the world. But I consider that the key driving force will be Love and Compassion. Without Love and Compassion the above ingredients may not yield the desired results. If the above ingredients are compared to the materialsrequired to bake a delicious pie, then Love and Compassion constitute the oven that bakes the pie. Thus, without the baking power of Love and Compassion the pie for living with peace, happiness and prosperity will not be possible. Here I will expound what Love and Compassion mean.

To derive the solution to any problem first we need to understand the nature of the problem in its totality, and down to its deep roots. If we do that, then we will find the solution easily. Because most of the time the solution for the problem lies within or close to the problem. That is why Albert Einstein said, *"If I were given one hour to save the planet, I would spend 59 minutes defining the problem and one minute to resolving it."* What is the universal problem the world is facing today starting from the individual level to the level of nations? **It is "conflict".** Conflicts of all kinds and dimensions are troubling the humanity at the individual level and at the global economic and geopolitical level so much that one wonders whether the mankind can ever attain peace, happiness, prosperity, and social justice. Therefore, many people do not believe that a solution can be found during their lifetime, and so they simply ignore all these and bury their heads deep up to their hearts in pursuing their own welfare ignoring their obligations to the society and to their fellow beings. This sets into motion a vicious cycle that adds to the very process of conflict. *By not making any attempts to understand the problem, knowingly or unknowingly people become part of the problem.*

So let us examine the problem called "conflict" and understand it in its totality and down to its deep roots. Late Jiddu Krishnamurthy, one of the greatest thinkers of the 20th century, who preached no religion, said *"You are the world. Human being is the whole. He is the society; he is the separate human being; he is the factor who brings about this chaos. He is the world, and the world is him.* ***So, if he changes, everything changes. If he does not*** *change, nothing changes.*" So, the problem appears to be simple and within our reach to fix, because we are the root cause of the chaos and disequilibrium in this world; yet we have been identifying the problem with external factors. Why are we failing to identify the problem properly and fix it? Again, Jiddu Krishnamurthy goes on saying *"We have got the capacity, the energy, the sufficient intelligence to go into ourselves, look at ourselves, face ourselves, never escaping from ourselves, we got all the energy to do that. But apparently when it comes to us, we become a kind of slack. Nobody is going to give it (a try). That is one absolute fact: irrefutable fact. We have leaders, we have teachers, we have saviors; we have every kind of outside agents.* ***And the misfortune is because we don't know ourselves, we are destroying other human beings. We are destroying this marvelous earth***."

Thus, although the mankind or humans or ourselves – you and me – can find the root cause of the chaos in the world, and can fix it, yet we do not do that because we do not know ourselves and so we destroy each other and the mother earth. How can this happen? It sounds absurd we destroy each other because we do not understand ourselves. But it is true, if we consider that we are all related and connected in one way or other in this world. Imagine that we are all like pearls in a beautiful necklace called the world, then each one of us is connected through an invisible thread that runs deep through ourselves and our hearts. If we understand that we are all connected to each other however distant we may appear in terms of worldly relations, through a common binding principle, then our vision of the world changes forever. We do not destroy each other, because we realize that if we destroy others, that hurts us also; because the same principle is binding us all together like a thread in the necklace called the world. If a necklace is damaged even at a single spot, all pearls can fall. This knowledge or understanding is the beginning of the Universal Love or love for all beings, which is far superior to the worldly or mundane love we see and experience in our day-to-day life.

Even mundane love can exist at different levels, depending on the mental maturity of the individual. As Erick Fromm, a German Philosopher and Professor of Psychology said: *Immature love says, 'I love you because I need you'; mature love says 'I need you because I love you'*. Both these forms of love are born out of ignorance of our true nature, which is the root cause of the chaos. Furthermore, these two forms of love, the mature and the immature, have a common denominator, the "need". Need is born out of selfishness, and any love based on selfishness inevitably leads to disappointment and sorrow when the selfish need is not fulfilled or does not exist anymore. Such a love lacks the clarity of vision we are all related to each other and hurting others will hurt us equally. Such a love is only an expression of our narrow vision or lack of understanding of ourselves. Just like only a lighted candle can light another candle, only a person who understands himself/herself in true sense can love others. Only such person can value the aspirations of others and respect them by cultivating Universal

Love. Today, due to the lack of such deep understanding and love we do witness a lot of conflicts at the individual level or even at the national level.

The solution for this malady is cultivating Universal Love. Universal Love is unconditional, and it is not based on 'need' for anything, because it needs nothing to sustain itself. Universal love sustains on the self-knowledge we are all connected to each other like the pearls in a necklace through a common principle. So, the Universal Love is a spontaneous expression of that self-knowledge and clear vision of the true nature of oneself. Such love manifests as an externally visible trait of "helping others always and hurting no one." The more and more of such manifestations of this trait occur at the individual level the more peace and prosperity we can witness in this world. Universal Love, which is not based on any 'need', never leads to disappointment or sorrow. Universal Love fundamentally differs from the worldly love in the sense it does not seek reciprocation. We need to understand that it is not the ability of a person to love that can lead to disappointment or sorrow. It is the expectation of that person that his/her love should be reciprocated. Thus, True Love is immune to disappointment or sorrow. Universal Love is so powerful, like a torch it illuminates its surroundings with the same feeling in others. All the great men and women of this world who touched the heart of the masses practiced the Universal Love.

Having defined or understood the meaning of the Universal Love, let us examine the Compassion. Merriam Webster dictionary defines compassion as "sympathetic consciousness of others' distress together with a desire to alleviate it". Thus, the definition of compassion has two parts or components. The first one relates to our consciousness as fellow humans. It is the sympathetic response from our hearts to the distress faced by our fellow humans. Among all the creatures, the humans are bestowed with the highest level of consciousness. So, as humans we should spontaneously feel for the distress of our fellow beings.

Compassion does not stop with the feeling. The second part of the definition of compassion states "with a desire to alleviate it". So, in true compassion, the spontaneous feeling comes with a desire to alleviate the distress in others, and it often results in a positive action. Otherwise, it is not true compassion; it only constitutes 'lip service'. Such lip service does no good. It is a form of self-deception. We often see lip service without a desire to alleviate the distress or positive action.

When a person is evolved to be conscious of the distress in others, but does not cultivate Universal Love, then what results is nothing but a combination of sympathetic face and lip service. Here the consciousness is clouded or delusional and it does not recognize the principle of Universal Love. If Universal Love is cultivated, then Compassion follows it like a shadow. This point can be exemplified by quoting not a philosopher or a religious leader, but a renowned scientist, Albert Einstein. He said: *"A human being is part of a whole, called the Universe, a part limited in time and* space. He experiences himself, his thoughts, and feelings, as something separated from the rest a kind of optical delusion of his consciousness. This delusion is a kind of prison for us, restricting us to our personal desires and to affection for a few persons nearest us. **Our task must be to free ourselves from this prison by widening our circles of compassion to embrace all living creatures and the whole of nature in its beauty**." Yes, in one way or other we are all prisoners.

As long as we are imprisoned by our limited consciousness, we can never realize the vastness of inner freedom and joy. Ever since the dawn of civilization, man is striving for all types of external freedom, such as political, economic, religious, industrial, technological etc. But if man does not attain inner freedom and realizes the value of Love and Compassion, he is not doing any good for himself or for the society. **As Dalai Lama said "Love and Compassion are necessities, not luxuries. Without them humanity cannot survive."**

Finally, one must understand that Love and Compassion should come with humbleness, especially if we are in high positions, wealthy or powerful. Otherwise, however hard we may try to cultivate Love and Compassion, they do not serve the purpose. As Nelson Mandela said *"Our deepest fear is not that we are inadequate. Our deepest fear is that we are powerful beyond measure. It is our light, not our darkness that most frightens us. There is nothing enlightening about shrinking so that other people won't feel insecure around us. And as we let our own light shine, we unconsciously give other people permission to do the same. As we are liberated from our own fear, our presence automatically liberates others."* If we can cultivate such a humble personality with Love and Compassion, there is nothing in this world we cannot accomplish. The great men and women of the world walked through this path and showed us the light. And if we are still groping in darkness, it is just due to our reluctance to follow the light – nothing more.

If you conduct yourself with Peace, Love and Compassion, then you are God.
- *Sri Sathya Sai Baba*

Plant the seeds of Love in your hearts. Let them grow into trees of Service and shower the sweet fruit of Ananda (Bliss). Share the Ananda with all.
- *Sri Sathya Sai Baba*

The heart with Compassion is the Temple of God.
- *Sri Sathya Sai Baba*

Human Creative Power
The Most Valuable Resource in the World

Photo by Swapnil Dwivedi on Unsplash

"...I believe that if you put all the creative power of human beings on one side and all the world's problems on the other, and put them into a battle, human creative power will always win. It's just that we don't use our creative power to address the problems; we use it to make money. How do we break from this?"
- Prof. Muhammad Yunus

Prof. Muhammad Yunus, winner of the Nobel Peace Prize in 2006 said: *"...I believe that if you put all the creative power of human beings on one side and all the world's problems on the other, and put them into a battle, human creative power will always win. It's just that we don't use our creative power to address the problems; we use it to make money. How do we break from this?"* (Cited from Harvard Business Review, December 2012, page 136). Prof. Yunus is 100% correct. No one could have articulated it better than Dr. Yunus about the value of human creative power in solving the problems faced by the humanity. Human creative power is a God-given gift to solve the problems of the world and thus benefit all humanity. In other words, God has empowered humanity to solve its own problems by using its own creative power. Yet, we tend to rely on a superpower or politicians or non-governmental organizations to solve the problems we "collectively" face. But we use our own creative intelligence "exclusively" to ensure **our own welfare and wellbeing.** This is the greatest irony or tragedy the humanity is facing and accustomed to these days, resulting in innumerable unsolved problems all over the world in all sectors of life – education, health, welfare, poverty, crime, social injustice etc.

It is a misconception to think that only a few people are blessed with creative intelligence or power, and these people are destined to become artists, architects, scientists, technologists, or innovators and entrepreneurs. Every human is blessed with creative intelligence or power. It is just being aware of it and channelizing it collectively to benefit the humanity. The more we learn of and channelize our creative power for the collective benefit, the more of it manifests and expands. But if we learn of our creative intelligence or power, but utilize it only for our personal benefit, then it will shrink eventually leading us into trouble. To some extent the current education system we have in India is responsible for this dichotomy in thinking. The educational system in India, barring a few privileged institutes, does not promote the inherent creative powers of the students. It rewards bookish knowledge more than creative power. Bookish knowledge without creative thinking to solve the problems of the humanity often ends up in pursuing personal agenda and welfare, without regard to the rest of the society. *We need an educational system that promotes both the intelligence and creative thinking with a compassionate approach to solve human problems.*

The life of Prof. Yunus itself is a perfect example of how human creativity can unfold and manifest if one utilizes it collectively to benefit the humanity. He said *"When I was doing my PhD and teaching, I had a bird's-eye view of the world. Then working in the village, door-to-door, person-to-person, I got a worm's-eye-view. I saw all the details. I could clearly see a problem and try to solve it. You start with 100 people, then move to the next 100. You gain bigger scale at a gradual speed. You're not designing at the outset for a million people. You're moving step-by-step rather than starting with a megastructure."* (Cited from Harvard Business Review, December 2012, page 136). The problem which Dr. Yunus could clearly see was - people at the bottom of the poverty cannot come out of it however hard they may struggle, because they just do not have the small amount of money needed to start a small business or learn a skill to come out of the poverty. And because of their utter poverty, they are not qualified for bank loans. To elevate such poor people, Prof. Yunus envisioned the microcredit and microfinance concept and established the Grameen Bank. This has been a very successful story, which helped millions of poor people, who would otherwise be left at the bottom of the poverty even in rapidly emerging economies. **Thus, a simple creative idea directed towards solving a mass social problem helped millions and made Prof. Yunus a world-renowned person.** *(http://en.wikipedia.org/wiki/Muhammad_Yunus)*.

Similarly, in 1970s at 58 years, after years of clinical practice and understanding the problem of blindness in India, Dr. Govindappa Venkataswamy envisioned that the business model of McDonald's, the American fast-food giant, can be adopted to solve the mega problem of blindness in India, which affects mostly the poor people. About 80% of the blindness can be preventable or curable. But the resources, such as doctors, nurses, hospitals, equipment, and the patient's paying capacity could not address the mass health problem in a country like India. So, Dr. Venkataswamy successfully adopted the McDonald's business model and addressed the problem of blindness in India. By training health care professionals thoroughly, adopting standard operating procedures (SOPs), in-house production of intra-ocular lenses, and establishing a high-throughput capacity with minimal resources, the Aravind Eye Hospitals and Clinics could perform high-quality, high-volume procedures in the time (10-fold higher than the national average) at a low cost or even free and thus created history. What started as 11-bed hospital has grown into a network of self-sustaining eye hospitals and clinics in India and the largest cataract facility in the world. Today, many major business schools all over the world discuss the model of Aravind Eye Hospital as part of their curriculum. Dr. Venkataswamy lived by the philosophy and belief that *"Intelligence and capability are not enough. There must be the joy of doing something beautiful."* The joy and beauty of his life is giving people back their lost vision. Video clip: http://www.youtube.com/watch?v=L045HMoHjS0

We may not be like Dr. Yunus or Dr. Venkataswamy; but there are many among us who could see a problem and either act or do not act creatively to solve the problem. We need to act creatively and compassionately when we see a problem, even when that problem does not affect us. Then only we identify ourselves with the rest of the humanity. What the humanity needs to solve its own problems is creative thinking and work. Emulating the examples of people like Drs. Yunus and Venkataswamy will solve the problems of the humanity and bless us with real peace and happiness. ***The greatest bliss one can attain is by serving the humanity utilizing one's own intelligence and creative power.***

Creativity is seeing what everyone else has seen, and thinking what no one else has thought. – Albert Einstein

Saving the Starfish: One at a Time

On a fine morning on the beach at sunrise and just when the tide receded, hundreds or thousands of starfish are stranded helplessly on the sand. Soon they would be eaten by the birds and other predators. Obviously, they needed help to go back to the water to survive.

Photo by Hoang Minh on Unsplash

A compassionate little girl, who understood the helpless nature of the starfish and felt the urge to save them, picked up the starfish and gently throwing them one at a time into the water. Ardently she was repeating this process. A young man, who was jogging on the beach, stopped for a few second and asked the little girl, "What are you doing with the starfish?" The little girl replied that she was helping the starfish survive, because they cannot go back to the water on their own. The young man told the little girl that as there were a lot of starfish on the beach, she could not possibly make a difference to them. Upon hearing that, the little girl gently threw another starfish into the water, and said, "I made a difference to this one" and then she smiled to the astonishment of the young man. This moved the young man so much he could not resist picking up a starfish and throwing it into the water before resuming his jogging. *Such is the impact the compassionate act of the little girl made on the mind of a young man.* Please watch this story on YouTube: https://www.youtube.com/watch?v=1wuSaNCIde4&feature=youtu.be&t=3

I am sure we all can appreciate the sublime and elevating message in the above story, especially after watching the video clip of it with the smiling little girl. But the million-dollar question here is, can we transform ourselves and act like that compassionate little girl in our day-to-day life? While we wish to do so, however, most of us find it not practical for various reasons. I can imagine at least two common reasons put forward by many whose hearts were tugged with this starfish story, but who were still reluctant to act. The first reason is the same as the young man expressed – *we cannot possibly make a difference because so many millions of people are in need in this world*. The second reason, often felt by those who consider that even a small difference is worth making is - *lack of time or wealth*. Here I would like to dissect these reasons and present compelling and rational or scientific argument these reasons are myths or born out of our own ignorance.

Let us first examine the argument *we cannot possibly make a difference because so many millions of people are in need in this world*. What if I ask a student who aspires to become a medical doctor: Why s/he wants to become a doctor? That person may tell that s/he wants to become a doctor to treat patients and alleviate their suffering. Then, if I say to that person "You cannot possibly make a difference because there are so many millions of patients in this world", then that person will react immediately saying "Yes, it is true there are millions of patients in this world; but I can make a difference in the lives of those patients I treat during my lifetime". Similarly, what will we hear if we pose the same question to a person who wants to pursue a profession that benefits the community directly or indirectly, such as a teacher, policeman, or a firefighter or a medical scientist? In all these cases, the answer will be the same: to educate as many students as possible (aspiring teacher) or catch as many criminals as possible (aspiring policeman) or save as many lives as possible from fire accidents (aspiring firefighter) or to invent as many new medicines as possible to cure diseases (medical scientist).

Interestingly, none of the above aspirant considers the absolute number of people they must tackle if they want to make a difference statistically. But they all consider only how much they can accomplish in their own lives is more important than the actual numbers in the world. However, ironically, the very people who display such a great spirit of service in choosing their professions often admit that they cannot make a difference in their personal ability to help others because there are so many millions suffering with poverty or disease in this world. Why this dichotomy in our lives? Because people see the suffering in this world through their own profession or lives and thus shape their responses to the suffering, they see around themselves. People do not see the suffering in the world in its totality or reality. However, they mentally expand their limited professional work to embrace the whole humanity in need. A doctor may think that s/he is alleviating the suffering of the patients while pursuing his/her profession and making a living out of it. The same is true for teachers or policemen or firefighters or even medical scientists. But once we take out 'making a living out of our own professions', very few of us will be left behind to serve the needy without seeking any return for their efforts. Despite this fact, we often think that we are serving the world with no selfish motive, while we are actually pursuing our own agenda and think that we are selflessly serving the world. But once we understand this logic, we may change, and we will serve without seeking return or remuneration for our effort. If we can do that, then we qualify ourselves for "nishkama karma" or 'selfless work' which Bhagawad Gita defined as a form of Yajna. The true meaning of Yajna is "an act directed to the welfare of others, done without desiring any return for it, whether of a temporal or spiritual nature" as per Gita (http://www.mkgandhi.org/momgandhi/chap46.htm). As per Gita, any act that does not constitute Yajna will entangle us in bondage and cycles of birth and death. It is understandable that one must pursue one's profession to make a living. But still one can dedicate at least certain amount of one's professional or personal time for doing Yajna and alleviate the suffering in this world using one's knowledge, skills and abilities and thus disentangle oneself from the karmic bondage. By doing so, one will also enrich one's life physically, mentally, intellectually, and spiritually. That brings more happiness into our lives than mere pursuit of our professions for a living.

Now, let us turn to the second reason often advanced by those who consider that even a small difference is worth making, i.e., **lack of time or wealth**. In real life, we may be busy and may not have enough wealth to take care of the needs of others. But research conducted by Dr. Zöe Chance and her colleagues Drs. Cassie Mogilner and Michael I. Norton, at the Yale School of Management, the Wharton School of the University of Pennsylvania, and the Harvard Business School are presenting compelling data to convince us that time and wealth are relative aspects in our lives depending on our mental perception. Their findings on the perception of time were first published in the journal *Psychological Science* (Giving Time Gives You Time, volume 23, pages 1223-1238, year 2012) and later defended by the lead author Dr. Cassie Mogilner in the Harvard Business Review (September 2012 issue, pages 28-29). The salient finding of this captivating study is **spending time helping others leaves people feeling as if they have more time, not less**. It may sound absurd, but it is true and is proven scientifically.

Briefly, in a battery of studies, these researchers assigned some test subjects (volunteers) to either help a person in need (e.g., writing a note for a sick child, or editing student's essay) or simply left them to do whatever they wanted (this group wasted their time doing things that benefit no other person). The outcome of the study was clear – in each experiment the people who lent a helping hand to others felt as if they had more time than the people who did not. What is the reason for this unexpected outcome of the study on perception of time? Dr. Mogilner explained "People who give time (to others) feel more capable, confident, and useful. They feel they've accomplished something and therefore, that they can accomplish more in the future. And this self-efficacy makes them feel that time is more expansive" (Harvard Business Review, September 2012 issue, pages 28-29). Perhaps this may be the reason we find people who are compassionate and often help others never say they are busy, whereas people who do not care to help others always utter "I am very busy".

Similar to the above published study on the perception of time, the research work of Dr. Zöe Chance and Dr. Michael I. Norton on wealth shows that people feel richer when they give money away. Their study results are intriguing and suggest that "just as acts of conspicuous generosity signal wealth and power to others, they trigger feelings of subjective wealth and power in those who give – despite decreasing their objective wealth" (Dr. Zöe Chance personal communication; please see below for full reference).

The above two studies, although originated in business schools, nevertheless, have profound meaning and application in philanthropy and altruism motivating people to share their time and wealth, however limited they may be. By doing so, people gain enormous subjective feeling of affluence in time and wealth, and thus enjoy confidence and satisfaction in their lives. This exalted state of mind is comparable to the expansive nature of human mind and self, aptly cited not by a philosopher, but a great scientist, Albert Einstein: *"A human being is part of a whole, called the Universe, a part limited in time and space. He experiences himself, his thoughts, and feelings, as something separated from the rest a kind of optical delusion of his consciousness. This delusion is a kind of prison for us, restricting us to our personal desires and to affection for a few persons nearest us. Our task must be to free ourselves from this prison by widening our circles of compassion to embrace all living creatures and the whole nature in its beauty."*

Acknowledgement: Thanks are due to Dr. Zöe Chance of the Yale School of Management for kindly sharing her research findings. **Reference: Chance Z et al, I Give, Therefore I have: Giving and Subjective Wealth.** (http://faculty.chicagobooth.edu/workshops/marketing/past/pdf/zoe%20chance.pdf)

Creating and Sustaining Balance:

Integrating Professional, Family, and Social Life

Photo by Jeremy Thomas on Unsplash

Most of us have three aspects of life – professional, family, and social. One of the toughest questions we all face is *"How to Create and Sustain Balance in Professional, Family and Social Life?"* There is no easy formula for it. It is such a complex issue, instead of working to create harmony or balance among the three aspects of our lives, most of us lead three compartmentalized lives. In this process, we sacrifice true inner happiness and peace in our lives, and instead pursue the fleeting joys of life, which are only mirages. The result is even the very successful people among us may not find the happiness or value in the worldly success they attained. Such people often lose the "chaitanya", which is a type of free-flowing consciousness that is the source of passion and life energy. *Why should it happen? Where are things going wrong? What can be done to avoid such a situation?* These are the toughest questions in life to address and find a solution. So, any amount of time spent to address these questions is worth every minute. Incidentally, I realized that I could come up with a "path", if not an "instant solution" for this problem. It is based on my own life experiences as well as the wisdom of other people.

As shown in the figure below, there are three main ingredients needed for a happy and balanced life. These are (i) living with a higher aim in life; (ii) value-added life; and (iii) love and compassion. It is important to develop and grow all the three ingredients to the same degree. There is little value in developing and growing one or two a lot and ignoring the others. Furthermore, it is essential we should try our best to integrate them into one. The more we integrate the three into one, the area where all three overlap (indicated by arrow in the right panel above) expands, and we develop peaceful and steady mind directly proportional to the area of this overlap. This is something one must experience by oneself, and it cannot be described in words.

But if we develop all the three ingredients, but not make any efforts to integrate them, then that leads to compartmentalized life without real peace and steadiness in our lives. Such a situation is comparable to having all the ingredients to bake a delicious pie, but not trying to make the pie. Then how can we experience the taste of a delicious pie? The ingredients needed to bake a pie are not pie themselves. *Baking the pie is the key here.* Now let us examine each of the three ingredients to understand what they mean and how to develop and grow them.

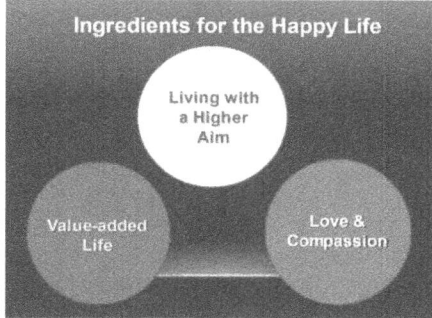 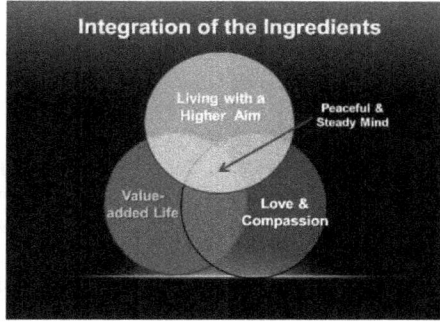

Living with a Higher Aim in Life: Most of us think that we have higher aims in our lives. But that may not be true always as quoted: *For most of us the problem is not that we aim too high and fail. It is just the opposite; we aim too low and succeed - Sir Ken Robinson.* That is true. Most of us aim lower than our inherent potentials, and then succeed easily and early in life. Our inherent potentials are like rubber bands. They can be stretched a lot. But we prefer to work comfortably without stretching them. So, naturally we set our goals lower than our full potentials. The result of aiming like that is life will cease to be challenging once we attain the success and its fruits, usually by our mid-life. If someone feels that s/he very successful in life, but does not find life challenging anymore, then that person might have been working on low aims in life.

The other issue is, since our childhood we have been told by our parents and teachers we should study well and become a doctor, engineer, lawyer, etc. We were coaxed to "find ourselves" by getting into one of these so-called great professions. But *Life is not about finding yourself. Life is about creating yourself - George Bernard Shaw*. That is true. We cannot attain real happiness in our lives if we just find ourselves. Finding ourselves is like re-inventing the wheel. Whether we find ourselves does not matter, because we are what we are. A wheel is a wheel. But one finds the value of a wheel only when one makes a cart or a car and mounts the wheel on to it. Similarly, it does not matter whether we are doctors or engineers or lawyers etc. All these professions are different types of wheels. What we do with those professions, and how we do is the key for a challenging and happy life. Thus, we need to create ourselves by transforming into better beings. But we may wonder that not all are creative in life, and those that are creative become artists, designers, architects or scientists. Again, that is a misconception: *...if you put all the creative power of humans on one side and all the world's problems on the other, and put them into a battle, human creative power will always win. It's just that we don't use our creative power to address the problems of life: we use it to make money. We need to break from this - Muhammad Yunus (Nobel Laureate in Peace, 2006).* God has blessed us all with creative power, but only a few of us use it to transform ourselves and solve the problems of life and the society and find happiness, whereas others misutilize their creative power and so do not find real happiness in life.

Money and Happiness: We should never make money as the goal in our life and then expect to be happy. That is like expecting for bright moonlight on a new moon day. Money is a means, but not the end of our lives. We may expect money to provide comforts, but not real happiness. Real happiness comes from things other than money. If someone thinks s/he is happy with money, then that person never tasted real happiness in life. Unless one experiences the real happiness, the person may easily get confused between "pleasure and comfort" and real happiness. Let us see what two of the world's richest persons, who appear to be very happy in life, say about money:

- *I can understand wanting to have a million dollars…. but once you get beyond that, I have to tell you, it is the same hamburger. - Bill Gates*

- *Making money isn't the backbone of your guiding purpose: making money is the by-product of your guiding purpose. - Warren Buffett*

Money is like a tool, which we should be able to use when we need and put it back in the toolbox and do other things when the repair work is done. We take it out when we need it, but unfortunately, we do not want to or do not know how to put it back when the work is done. The result is it gets stuck or even "super glues" to our hands and minds and thus makes them useless for doing better things in life. The glued tool in our hands and minds will also hurt the people around us, including our own family members. It is a common observation that people who are deeply attached to money do not realize the value of any other thing, including the value of other people who are not crazy about money, and thus mess up with their own lives. Money can severely handicap our ability to enjoy life in its true sense. Money can also make us feel like we are "special" thus breeding a sense of class, by which we lose our natural inclination of love and compassion for all beings. One evil often associated with making money as the goal in life is comparison with others who are richer. This practice eventually leads to loss of happiness in life. Again, let us see what one of the richest men on earth says about this anomaly.

- *I just naturally want to do things that make sense. In my personal life too, I don't care what other rich people are doing. I don't want a 405-foot boat just because someone else has a 400-foot boat. Happiness comes within. Live simple life. Find happiness in simple pleasures. - Warren Buffett*

All these prove only one thing. *The money per se does not lead to loss of happiness, but the attitude of the person possessing money that deprives happiness.* So, just as we smear our hands and knife with oil before we cut open a jack fruit and take out the delicious kernels, so also, we need to "smear our minds with wisdom" and make them non-sticky before we think about making money. Otherwise, our minds can become as sticky and messy as our hands if we attempt to cut open a jack fruit without smearing them with oil. That is the secret of life.

Value-added Life: This is another key ingredient for creating and sustaining happiness in professional, family, and social I have elaborately described about value-added life in another section. We look for value in everything we buy or acquire; but we fail to realize that we should cultivate values in our own lives, so the society finds value in us. The above comparison illustrates what is meant by value-added life vis-à-vis with a valuable car we wish to purchase.

The Value of a Car we want to buy	The Value we need to Cultivate for ourselves
• Brand name & dependability • Turbo-charged horse-power (HP) • Traction control (TC) • Electronic stability control (ESC) • Anti-lock braking system (ABS) • 6-8 Airbags SRS • Large room for co-passengers	• Credibility & Integrity • Strong motivation and drive (HP) • Intellectual grip (TC) • Perfect mental balance (ESC) • Capacity to avoid locking into unwanted issues (ABS) • 6-8 Virtues that can deploy like airbags in a crisis (SRS) • Large heart to accommodate others' needs.

Love and Compassion: The true source of happiness in life is love and compassion towards all beings. The natural inclination of humans is love and compassion for all, which generates inner happiness. This is reflected in every infant and child. But the selfishness breeds and grows within as the child grows that destroys love and compassion, and thus leads to gradual loss of inner happiness. The result is people look for happiness in external things they can buy with money. This is only trying to quench the thirst by going after mirages on a hot sunny day – a futile exercise. Cultivation of love and compassion and its expansion into our family, professional and social lives will give us immense happiness and satisfaction. The earlier we realize this fact in our lives, the better for us and for the society. I have elaborately dealt with love and compassion in another section. Here are a few points to ponder.

- Life is nothing but a bridge between birth and death – we need to cross it.
- We have to share the bridge with others with love and compassion.
- We make a living with what we get, and we make a life with what we give.
- Good and evil are the projections of our mind only.
- Love and compassion will take us to God than any prayer.
- A loving and compassionate heart is the key for peaceful living.

Diamond versus Graphite: Diamond and graphite (coal) are made of the same element, the carbon. But the former is rare and very valuable, and latter is in abundance and is very cheap.

Cut and polished diamonds are mounted on precious gold jewels. But coal ends up as fuel in factories or thermal stations or in cooking pits. What gives such a value to diamond as compared to the graphite is not its elemental composition, but the internal structure and strength of the chemical bonding among the carbon atoms. Similarly, what differentiates people of nobility from the rest is their inner strength and integrity, not external appearance, or riches. Just like the brilliance of a diamond comes from the light it scatters, not the light it absorbs, so also the value we generate in our lives comes from what we give to this world, but not what we take from it. We should all try to live like diamonds in this world and thus derive happiness from that noble act. Interestingly, most of us have that inherent potential to live like diamonds. But we might not have realized that potential. It is similar to the fact that out of the four Cs that make a diamond precious - *carat, clarity, color and cut* - the first three are dictated by nature. It is only the *cut* that requires human skill. The value of even a modest sized raw diamond increases enormously by proper cutting and polishing in the hands of skilled diamond cutters. Conversely, a badly cut diamond, even if it is large, may not show a marked increase in its value. Similarly, we need to mold and transform ourselves properly to show our value to the world and thus derive happiness. But our inherent potential, however enormous it may be, has no value to the world if we fail to transform properly in the right way. Without that transformation, we may not realize the true value and happiness in our lives. Such a transformation also needs great inner strength.

Life is a song - sing it.
Life is a game - play it.
Life is a challenge - meet it.
Life is a sacrifice - offer it.
Life is love - enjoy it.
  - Sri Sathya Sai Baba

Sanathana Dharma

Photo by Navneet Shanu from Pexels

Sanathana Dharma, often loosely translated as "ancient wisdom", is a set of principles that guide the humanity and human destiny. No one knows who authored these principles. But they have been propagated over several millennia in India and other parts of Asia and percolated into Asian religions and philosophies.

It is widely believed that Sanathana Dharma, which predates Hinduism, is the root of Hinduism. Some scholars believe that Sanathana Dharma is the original name of Hinduism, as the word Hindu is an ethno-geographical *term* and does not refer to a religion. Nowhere in the scriptures, including the Vedas, the word Hindu can be found.

Persians, who could not pronounce Sindh, used to say Hindu when they referred to the land currently covered by the river Sindh (Punjab and Pakistan). Eventually the people living in this region came to be known as Hindus, with no implication to their religion. Thus, one can equate Sanathana Dharma to the ancient wisdom of India, with no religious tones or implications. Depending on which scripture or literature or school of thought one follows, the number of principles of Santhana Dharma vary widely. But for all practical purposes, it is often identified with five principles, namely Satya (Truth), Dharma (right conduct, approximate translation), Santhi (Peace), Prema (Love) and Ahimsa (non-violence). The beauty of these five principles is they run in tandem when one practices Sanathana Dharma, but they are synergistic. For instance, without first practicing Satya, a person cannot even understand Dharma. Only a person who practices Satya rigorously will see the nature of Dharma. Similarly, without understanding Dharma, a person cannot experience Santhi. Without Santhi, one cannot manifest and cultivate Prema for all beings. Only when Prema is installed in the heart, the person can understand Ahimsa and its implications for spiritual progress. So, when Satya or Truth is the first casualty, then that person cannot progress on the path of Sanathana Dharma, despite of doing all possible religious rituals and reciting all slokas. Mere understanding of these five principles will not help a person to progress on spiritual path. One must immerse oneself in these eternal principles and live up to their true meaning. Then only a person can be considered as practicing Sanathana Dharma. Unfortunately, many people do not understand these facts and ignore Satya, the first step in the path.

Why so much importance is given to Satya in Sanathana Dharma? It is simple. God is Truth. By negating Satya, one negates the God. If we do not speak Truth, then there is no use. It is because, we cannot advance even an inch toward God without being truthful. God manifests only when there is truthfulness. The moment with God. That is why Satya is the first step toward Godhead.

Once Satya is taken care of, Dharma will sprout within us. Dharma is very subtle, and it needs clarity of intellect to understand it and follow. Without following Satya ardently, one cannot even grasp Dharma. There is no equivalent word for Dharma in any language, not just in English. It is often translated as the "right conduct". But Dharma is much more than that. It is intertwined with our actions toward others and in this world. It is dictated by our inherent nature, which can get clouded easily if one is not following truthfulness. The current day chaos in the world we see around due to the lack of Dharma is the result of lack of truthfulness by the people. So, to understand Dharma and follow it, one must practice Sathya.

Once a person can grasp Dharma and follows it ardently, then that person experiences real inner Santhi. But people who understand the Dharma often hesitate to act on the right path, because they may likely to lose something worldly or materialistic by following Dharma. This is the litmus test that Dharma administers to everyone. If one wants to follow Dharma, one must be prepared to lose anything for it. It is a sacrifice that is worth for the progress of the Soul. But people do not realize that fact and their attachments to material objects or wealth or even family members make them knowingly shun from Dharma. But if one can pass this litmus test, one will reach higher realms of spiritual progress by gaining Santhi or inner peace, which no amount of worldly wealth or riches can buy.

Once a person experiences Santhi or inner peace, then that person develops inner strength to follow Dharma. At this point a person experiences a synergy between Dharma and Santhi. The more Santhi one gains, the more strength one gets to follow Dharma. That will boost the Santhi or experience of inner peace. At this stage a person develops a strong intellect to detach himself/herself from what the world thinks about them and thus follow the inner light or guidance.

The Santhi or inner peace also blesses a person with Prema or the ability to love all beings, whether they are his kith and kin or even his adversaries. This is the Universal Love that will save the humanity from conflicts or violent acts. The Universal Love or Prema will bestow the person with the ability to follow the path of Ahimsa or non-violence, the highest point in Santhana Dharma. Ahimsa does not mean weakness. It takes more courage to display Ahimsa than committing a violent act. The power of the Soul manifests through Ahimsa.

Another beautiful thing about Sanathana Dharma is its principles are universal. These five principles are found in all major religions. Thus, it appears Sanathana Dharma predates all known religions and may as well be the fountainhead of all religions

Swadharma vs. Paradharma

Picture: Courtesy of Wikimedia Commons

*śreyān swa-dharmo viguṇaḥ para-dharmāt sv-anuṣhṭhitāt
swa-dharme nidhanaṁ śhreyaḥ para-dharmo bhayāvahaḥ*

In Bhagwad Gita, in Karma Yoga (Chapter 3), verse 35, looking at Arjuna in a state of despondency and was not willing to wage a war against his cousins, elders and peers, Lord Krishna revealed about the nature of Swadharma and Paradharma as follows. *One's own Dharma, though imperfect, is better than the dharma of another well discharged. Better death in one's own dharma; the dharma of another is full of fear.* (From the commentary by Swami Chidbhavananda, Sri Ramakrishna Tapovanam).

The above lines have a profound meaning and relevance today than 5,000 years ago when they were uttered by a Lord Krishna. Swadharma literally translates into one's own dharma. Paradharma means the dharma of another. But not that simple as the literary translation. When Lord Krishna uttered these words, He was referring Swadharma to the inherent nature of a person. But over the past 2,000 years, due to the rigid structure of caste system that evolved in India, people, and even scholars interpreted Swadharma as Kula Vrithi or the profession by Caste of family lineage. For instance, they interpreted that the Swadharma of the son of a farmer is farming, that of a son of merchant is trade, and that of a son of the priest is priesthood. That is not what Lord Krishna meant. The inherent nature of Arjuna is to stand up and fight for the righteousness and protect the people from the wicked. He never hesitated to do that, and won many battles, killing several wicked people. But when the ultimate challenge came at Kurukshetra, where he had to face his cousins, uncles, grandparents, and guru, he was shrinking and backing of from fulfilling his obligatory duty or Swadharma. Instead of waging a heroic war, he wanted to quit his ambition for kingdom, which he and his brothers cherished for the 14 years when they were exiled in the forests, and for which they did penance and acquired mighty weapons from the gods. By quitting to fight, Arjuna will not gain anything good in his life. He may fall from his destiny. That is when Lord Krishna explained to him the nature of Swadharma and Paradharma and the two results they will yield by following them. A man's journey in life is to attain liberation from all actions and fears, but not to get entangled into the actions and fears. Only by following the Swadharma, however hard or imperfect it may be, man can attain liberation from all actions and fears. But by following Paradharma, just because it looks more attractive or better, or even easier, man falls from his path to liberation from all actions and fears.

To understand the philosophical and spiritual logic behind the above explanation, we need to first understand human bodies and transmigration of souls from one body to another after death. According to our scriptures, humans have five bodies (Koshas) as follows. The Annamaya Kosha or the gross body which nurtures on the food and water and sustains on them. It is made of the gross elements and chemicals that go down into the earth when our bodies decay or cremated. The next inner layer, which is subtler than the Annamaya Kosha is Manomaya Kosha. This makes our mind. Although it is subtler than the Annamaya Kosha, still it is part of this physical world and ceases to exist at death. The third layer, more subtle is Pranamaya Kosha, which provides the energy needed to run the other two Koshas and keeps the person alive. If Annamaya Kosha is like the hardware, the Manomaya Kosha is the software. But, just like a computer needs hardware, software and the power or electricity, the Annamaya and Manomaya Koshas need Pranamaya Kosha to be alive and work together. Just like the Annamaya and Manomaya Koshas, the Pranamaya Kosha belongs to the physical world, similar to the electricity, although we cannot see or define it like a material. All these three Koshas cease to exist at death and disintegrate or dissipate into the surroundings. The other two Koshas, which are even subtler, persist after death and move to a new body at the next birth. The fourth one is Vijnyanamaya Kosha or the body of superior knowledge we gained in this and previous births. It should not be confused with the information we gathered from the books or media. It is the gist of all realizations and deep understandings we obtained during the sojourn of soul through different bodies. Vijnyanamaya Kosha also moves between the physical and metaphysical world, directing our thoughts and actions during the wakeful time, and connecting to the other worlds during sleep. It is more like the Internet connection to a computer. We use the internet and download information into our computer or upload files from our computer to the Internet, but the internet is not part of our computer (physical body). The Vijnyanamaya Kosha is like the "seed", which determines which type of birth we will have next time. The final one is Anandamaya Kosha, or the body of bliss. This is the Eternal Soul or our true nature, although different schools identify Anandamaya Kosha differently. Only the Vijnyanamaya Kosha and Anandamaya Kosha persist after death. The Vijnyamaya Kosha will also disintegrate once the individual soul attains liberation or merges with the Cosmic Soul. Even the Annandamaya Kohsa does not exist as a separate entity.

Just like a doll made of salt going into the sea and dissolves into it with no trace of its identity, at liberation, the Anandamaya Kosha merges with the Cosmic Soul of the God.

Now let us examine how the above translates into Swadharma and Paradharma. At the time of death, the Vijnyamaya Kosha that contains the gist of all knowledge, realizations and deep understanding gained in this and previous births is like a "seed" that determines the nature of the next birth. So, when a child is born, there is this seed of Vijnyanamaya Kosha deep in it. It will be dormant for many years until that child attains a certain age when the seed manifests in the thoughts of the child. This seed directs the child to choose its destiny in this world, unfold its inherent potentials fully in a healthy way and thus allow it to attain perfection in life. It is like the seed of a flowering plant, be it a rose or jasmine or marigold, which determines only that plant will sprout and the flowers will blossom. If that child may manifest itself as per the inherent seed in it, then it is following Swadharma.

So far, so good; as long as the child is free and allowed to manifest its inherent seed and unfold its mind and intellect, then it is following its Swadharma. But that does not happen always, especially in countries like India, or in most Indian families anywhere in the world. Due to the possessiveness of the parents, who would love to shape the destiny of their children, and the social pressures, a child does not have the time and inclination to understand and manifest its inherent seed. It is constantly pushed to choose a profession or life which the parents are interested as it may boost their image or family prestige, a notion based on wrong beliefs. In this process, often the child, which is destined to become X by the nature of its inherent seed, may end up becoming Y. It is like a rose plant is forced to blossom marigolds or vice versa. In this process, a child may or may not be happy, but its inner nature is affected, as the Vijnyanamaya Kosha is not perfectly aligned with other Koshas. More important, it is also possible, that a child that is destined to become an outstanding performer and achiever in a particular field based on the nature of its inherent seed, may become less than outstanding in the new field it is manipulated to take up. This will never be known to us. What we know is a large proportion of youth in India (15 to 29 years) are suffering from depression, with a suicidal rate that tops the world. Definitely there is some discordance in their hearts and minds. It has nothing to do with socioeconomic conditions, as it is seen among all sections of students. Whether that is due to the parental pressure to excel in studies or choose a profession of their choice is not known but needs to be considered within the context of Swadharma and Paradharma. In addition, some youth are choosing professions based on the formula of number of years of study vs. starting pay, but not based on their inherent seeds. While these are apparently happy, it is difficult to sustain that happiness on long-term basis, as the urge of their inherent seeds to sprout on their own is never understood and is suppressed. Conversely, it is obvious that in cultures where the children may choose their destiny as per their inherent nature or seed, the number of outstanding performers or high achievers or legendary figures in different professions is much higher. The best example is Jewish community, who constitute 0.2% of world population, but have 18% share in Nobel prizes. This is something Indians must contemplate and evaluate whether they are doing the right thing or not.

Although in ancient times India was leading in science, technology, and medicine, today, despite of an intelligent population, the contribution of Indians to science, technology and medicine is very poor or dismal. Mere brains won't help to become high achievers making outstanding contributions in any field. The inherent seed or the Vijnyanamaya Kosha must align property with other Koshas and the destiny of the soul. Finally, those Indians, with the liberty and choice to allow their inherent seeds sprout freely without parental or societal influence, are unfortunately making money as their ultimate goal in their life. This is a wrong approach, as by doing so, they cannot leave their current bodies with a better Vijnyanamaya Kosha than they were born with. Instead of making money their goal, they should take up a cause or a problem to solve in their lives. By doing so, they will make a better inherent seed for their next birth and thus move forward toward the path of liberation. Thus, the concept of Swadharma and Paradharma preached by Lord Krishan to Arjuna 5,000 years ago, is very relevant today. And we need to understand it in its true sense.

If we go by the laws of the physical, it will always be governed by boundaries. If we want to experience the boundless nature of the non-physical, we need to turn inward and follow the way of Swadharma. - Sadhguru

www.ingramcontent.com/pod-product-compliance
Lightning Source LLC
Chambersburg PA
CBHW060223050426
42446CB00013B/3148